ROOM TONE

poems by

Vanessa H. Smith

Finishing Line Press
Georgetown, Kentucky

ROOM TONE

ACKNOWLEDGMENTS

"infrequent diaper changes" was published in *Topical Poetry*

"Today My Daughter" was published in *Silent Auctions Magazine*

"A Woman of Three Ways" was published in *Chronogram*

"He Asked Me Once, We Married Twice" was published in *On the Seawall*

"California Dry Tethered" was published by *Tiny Seed Literary Journal*

"Inventive" was published in *Poetry Apocalypse*

Publisher: Leah Huete de Maines
Editor: Christen Kincaid
Cover Art: Russell and Vanessa by Annette Fox Smith
Author Photo: Robin Parish
Cover Design: John Kramer

Order online: www.finishinglinepress.com
also available on amazon.com

Author inquiries and mail orders:
Finishing Line Press
PO Box 1626
Georgetown, Kentucky 40324
USA

Contents

The Beginning Seams of January 1

To Where Dailyness 2

He Has Always Been a Bird 3

Stripping a Bed 4

infrequent diaper changes 5

Today My Daughter 6

A Woman of Three Ways 8

He Asked Me Once, We Married Twice 9

Beach House 10

Kathmandu 12

In the Hospital 15

TREES, and Besides Us 17

California Dry Tethered 18

the picture as interview 19

House Fire in Chile 20

An About to be Cremated Swimmer 22

My Mother-in-Law's Shower 23

Five Different Painters' Lines 25

Inventive 26

for Russell Dymock Smith
Donald Alan Weeden
Andrea Henderson Fahnestock
and
Jack Dymock Russell Antoville Matisse Picasso Pink
November Smith Eucalyptus Hedwig Fox Weeden

"One does not discover new lands without consenting to lose sight
of the shore for a very long time."
Andre Gide

"A goal is a dream with a deadline."
WONTON Golden Bowl Fortune Cookie Company

The Beginning Seams of January

into palm, psalm, and olive,
purity and extracts grown from inactive places are
forced into action,
while far-flung foreign markets
seem stripped and cleared from their born constitution.

the beginning of capability is
to pronounce words, jump freedom—
solid and paper-like at the same time.
states of mind, proposed, remain held together
with pins and glue.

some people are born in, and run at January.
the fear of winter weather might make them sturdy and
excellent creatures,
or not.

now this, another January has come again
on the heels of hushed discussion.
the idea is to dismount at once.

To Where Dailyness

To where I wiped daily dabs of lipstick on the car carpet, it saturated
and made a hole
To where the rolling wave held something back in response to sand,
and the man decided he didn't need to be saved
To where my brother stuffed a napkin full of chewed eggplant under
the table, the healthiest meals tasted the worst
To where my father's thoughts drifted at the long dinner table, to
examine his sister's sad eyes
To where the fear of fighting drifted into sleep on Monday nights, and
the deal would have to wait until the next day
To where the argument got boiled down, softening into snoring and
slumber, and the telephone rang just one more time
To where the ambulance lights reflected on the ceiling from the street
below, and each time the siren sang, a prayer was sent out
To where a tree decides to let go and die, as urban planners forget to notice
To where the roots of my hair turn a slight gray, and their easy attitude
as they pull away from youth
To where the dictionary falls open to reveal a new navigation, and the
car careens into the boulder
To where the orchestra fades to ballet steps, and poaches the night
To where the house sits undusted and forlorn waiting for children, and
the curry holiday stew was never to be served again

He Has Always Been a Bird—A History of Motherhood Finished

My eyes are dark walnuts. No one to care and fen for.
One night, the package of him flies away on a plane to his first
separate home. West.
I had already dreamt that I was buried, ended,
between two saddles the color of
cypress tree green. Uploaded anguish.

Our body worries me. He will need a dentist, a doctor,
in the land of California fire. Alone.

He is a tiny sculpted piece—the best part that came of me—
motherhood a passage,
that began when newly separated at birth, I saw him lying down,
our dark wet commingled hair the same.

It has always been for him that I digest the world
and offer up the softest curated bits.

Stripping a Bed—"He" of the World—My Son

I would rather not strip
the bed after he leaves,
this" he" of the world,
my man - son is not five any longer.
his hair is short cut and
his body a longing leanness.

he was a tiger baby born small, concise,—
uniforms played on him through
all his games.

we rode planes loaded with his cargo.
plastic bottles filled with milk
performed their duty
in practical order,—
their pure
white splendor
he drank
and grew.

he deftly steered away from the
personality of mistakes and crime.
instead, he listened to
the free song of the west
and the heights of a city
where he now lives.

there are toothpicks on the floor of his room.
I don't want to think about his teeth
or the toenails I just cut,
cropped close and clean
or the way the bath smells after he showers.

I have lost the little in him—
the being born time
when he needed me.
thankfully, he now greets the world he was invited to, and
eager—project complete.

infrequent diaper change

what is it to be urban?
fire
as it blares, while you see yourself streak down the street,
showing your swagger,
women talon vodka in coke bottles with straws
assembled in short mini-skirts.

if babies don't have their diapers changed often enough
both mother and child may suffer mentally.
meanwhile the shortage of baby formula
remains in America while,
that other world of money stays opaque—
a sea foam monster
swimming like a slippery eel in the dark.

a gas leak comes to mind.

and one man passing by said,
"I think liquidity is a good idea now."

Today My Daughter

Today my daughter swore it
would be the last day of her being pretty.
She looks at her face and its drowsy make-up application
and how habits die wide.

Her face broadens and hides any ill motive
like a rose-lit moon
drawn on a sky of glass.

Her eyelids close
the world down at night.

Today my daughter swore that
her birthday was falling all
around her.
I made a cake of crimson roses
topped with a tall frosted fortune.
Crumbs of moistened bites were
translucent, and warming.

Today my daughter
imagines she is crowned
President of Kindergarten
before she makes
her farewell speech
and moves along.

After watching the moon
travel through the night, she is
awake now,
frightened by sounds
out of doors.

Today my daughter wants to be re-born
in India.
She knows that if she waits too long
the world might change its mind, brittle up to
let her slip back

into the waters.

A Woman of Three Ways

Her body silhouettes as tall thin college age glass
Character in a body of left frames
Inside body the line a see-through hint
Napkins get wet body sweat and sand

He speed bumped hard over her
A broad body of water and marriage
Small branched body arms and one leg

Her thin railing body succumbed to divorce
Body pedestal bed other language
Later she will bend down in ballet soft foam

He Asked Me Once, We Married Twice

My kayaker boyfriend wrote out the proposal for me to check one box—yes? no? maybe? on a SWEET N' LOW packet.

With time to spare the morning of the first wedding, a few of my friends and I watched glass bead necklaces threaded in the bazaar.

Late morning the travel agent threw a fit with one of our travelers and I had to intervene.

The wedding was planned to take place in a monastery that very same November Nepal afternoon and I almost missed it.

My mom had asked if he got my engagement ring from a box of Cracker Jacks—a compliment since my favorite tiny plastic doll came from a long-ago box.

Number two wedding would be official so again I had to think about it carefully.

I happened to be invited to an ayahuasca ceremony in the west village—and took the opportunity to ask the big question again— should I marry him? I thought I was too young.

Full of hallucinogenic ayahuasca, I dreamt I was drowning, He rescued me by gently lifting me to the water's surface to breathe.

The second wedding was planned outside in Central Park but it rained and we ended up being married in Pandora's Box, by a man who married people who were not baptized.

Unprepared to read our ceremony in a dark room, the minister lit a match to see the poem studded nuptials,—my only copy—he almost burned them all then and there.

Beach House

A bed in his
wife's beach house
a walk down the hall
to my boyfriend's bedroom
where we stayed overnight.
I knew I was sleeping
with the wrong man
having met the couple's daughter
who held her house
in her mouth.
The daughter would not have
that type of dinner
many other nights.
She would learn to choose a parent
over the other,
unsure where divorce
would land her.
Interruptions that night and
conversation that led to more
months later that same bed
full of sand
had to be cleared with this separated man.
I made three types of fish salad—
wife in France with daughter
and wife would return to this
her one summer bed
in the summer house,
more single than when she had left.
It took hours to make that bed
retrieve a lost earring, foolhardy, stealing
he stole
I stole.

I have tried to call him once
his second and writer wife
wouldn't want to hear my voice.
      I apologize to the air and birthdays
      and the way I think and celebrate
keep going
passing by Hamptons,
I never knew how far away I had been.

Today I took a shower
like that day I dreamt his baby ripple inside, a small salmon
swimming upstream   for her life.

KATHMANDU

Buddha has lived here
and does still.

I became a newlywed
then—in this place, with little purchase.
my husband had lived here before with his precious girlfriend
who drowned in a river.
the road she was driving along
collapsed and
left her no way to escape.
she has an identical twin sister.

just inside our small home,
decorated in pink and red,
there was a place reserved for
watching over the dead.
I became a discoverer
twice, there.

Things that animals do not notice:
That they are being considered for sacrifice
That their owners are hungry
That they may become food

one day I was asked to join a tour group
traveling from America
to visit a Tibetan doctor.
I knew the group's leader—
he was also an author
who wrote about forbidden waterfalls,
hidden mountains,
and secrets.

I did not know what to expect.
this doctor called on each of us to
approach her
as one by one she quietly identified
our affliction
—sucked out blood and hair and bits of gristle through our skin,
which she spat out into a big silver bowl.
one woman had breast cancer.

I was the last to be treated,
didn't have to identify my "area of illness."
without a word, the doctor unzipped my pants
and sucked near
my right ovary.

when I got home, I stripped and
took a picture of myself in the mirror.
teeth marks and a big oval showed up.

that same week, I had asked the local butcher
about when he would
need more meat.
the day before I had noticed that two goats
waited, tethered behind his shed.

I asked to film the procedural slaughter
as I imagined it would be fascinating.

what I saw then
was an hour-long dance of the greatest precision
like surgery done in open air—
starting with the neck being slit
while the goat was still held by the rope.
after the head came off, the body shook.
a bit later, the body crumpled
to the ground.

the butcher split the animal open lengthwise
and opened it like a book,
took various organs out,
separating them into bowls.
last were the long beads
of intestine.
they were a lighter pink
compared to other parts.
blood was at a minimum, and
also put into a separate bowl.

this was 30 years ago
the most startling violence of this—
the thing I remember most of all
left to watch
the second goat still tied to the rope.

In The Hospital

Again, my nurse makes sure I am who she thinks I am.
Yes, I am Frankenstein being wheeled to new life.
I examine my body in the last bathroom I use before surgery.

It is still my body—¾ view slender,
still me, as of yet uninterrupted, uncut, and not quite breaking.

The hallway is a sea of voices talking about barbeque lunch,
about giving money to a boy who came to the ER alone
and is about to leave,
the same way,
but with more money.
One talkative nurse organizes a collection for him.
I see mine rushing away with green dollars in her hand.
The nurses are stewardesses riding unworried in major turbulence.
They strike portrait poses and keep moving in beauty.

Flowers convert the makeshift quality of hospital rooms
while bodies come and go.
In area—BED 12, just the semi-opened drapes
provide me visual sanctuary, and a lonely belonging.
The nurses continue asking who we all are.
They have asked me too.
My body has still felt like my own.

Meanwhile the patient,
in a hopeful soapy state of mind,
tries to jigsaw together
practicality, and the unseen
with an overlay of belief,
requisite for being a patient
and a positive outcome.

A bouquet-less room,
settles in to wait for new patients.
Nurses and doctors don't really notice
how bland hospital rooms are.

They are doing the important work.
Some rooms are filled to overflow with gifted blossoms—
carnations, delphiniums, and drawn out
sunflowers, outlined against dull white walls.
Nurses and staff clean all things
might leave flowers untouched,
as if they were corsages for a faraway debutante's wrist.

TREES, and Besides Us

perhaps the only thing that should
stand on earth
are
trees
pulling gum and gravity down
burying for us
roots far below—like stem cells
to volunteer

for now
trees punctuate through time and sky
they
sink garbage
mistress
concerns
as they stand directly beside us

I know of a place where the town raped a forest
to devise a building
done and dug out with caterpillars and earth movers
to remove and ground stumps before
people could examine just how much of the world
was spilt open and
destroyed

trees hold up the knife and fork of fairy tale
become lounge chairs for dreams
the high priestess justice judges while
—something stolen in the night
often happens when trees are still awake

they signal
we are no longer inside their world
although we hide amongst them
the embedded spirits of deceased
totem poles, skyscrapers
eucalyptus
the beginnings of our names for all those things

California Dry Tethered

The radio plays back
as she named me after an opera.
My mother painting me again
again.
I was her easiest model,
for practicing various lives on a face.
I treasure these paintings—the ones in which she recognized herself at
work
and in the visible.

Without her to drag through the sunshine, I hug along the coast to ride
the pearl.
We used to glance together at the shutter just as it closed, the graphic
before things rose
in the sunsetting skies.

Some glints of paint and zirconium asphalt spill into their own poem.
California—its contents stay dry—like
the window dressing and restraint it must take not to sweat.
Only paintings know these secret things.

The opposite is opposition.
Old dry nails hammered slightly into white plaster walls.
My mother's paintings hang precariously and
could fall any time.

We wait, we dry out into plaster, and become the wall.
The dry and cold of a California I never mastered is coming back in
plumes
of hot pink, pueblo orange, and chartreuse yellow smile color.
My friend, a horse whisperer of plants, notices nearby piles of cacti
carcasses
left out in the air,—they cling to the ground, lay, garnish, attempt.

the picture as interview

my mother painted portraits
of me at all stages,
ages, colors, emotions,
on various edges.

in one picture, the story circling out
is from a recent hospice episode
with my father-in-law.
my face looks flotsam green and
shiny like his final face.

my face, like an interview,
tells the most important
stories first—
the insane asylum and conversations I
had with its jolly residents
on a French hillside
etcetera.

stories from my light green eyes,
my silver city pink lips are
about a step, in life, in the middle
of a week, a year, a decade—
framed like a pebble in my palm
to talk about if someone asks or
looks at a picture of my face.

House Fire in Chile

Orange catches against blue sky
Ash escapes
To stash itself, small at first
on the dry wooden roof

My husband pours water on the burning logs below
as I run for help
Screaming all the way through wet grass
Thinking to ask for water that would be nowhere found

Fire moves like an Olympian
Stroking, engaging large licks in fast time
Moving through in single strong mouthfuls
Smoke of thick unfurling cream—a beautiful shade
I only noted
Once, as it grabbed at the living room ceiling
The upstairs now invisible to the eye
One small piece of burning ceiling sat on the couch

The entryway was the last standing piece to fall
Arched and open as if two people's fingers were intertwined
holding one another together in air
welcoming

On the inside too
Newly unpacked groceries
Bottles of wine and chili, a tweezer in its package
Rooms that would not be used for their original purpose again
But would still hold some former shape

My small tubes of un-used paint
Once burned, had made flattened marshmallow shaped 1960s flowers
Hollow, light weight silver. Silver and black.

The house became the size of an eyelash
Nighttime fell around the day
Controlled by nothing, at all

Fire is a movie of sorts
Sifting through the burned debris after
I found 4 tin cups and one Nature
Magazine
Some of those images I shaped and photographed lying there

Then later on, I remembered and thought
especially for my husband and son,
Wash your face
Be a poem

Glance back
The land is still there

And where I come from originally
You can still see from the peninsula
A spectacular daring of rock face

An About to be Cremated Swimmer

My face broadcasts this fine swimmer
as well as my dead parents
Their pouches and translucent strands
Who appreciated food, beauty, birds, and the earth
Until the end

My eyes cried and split
My father-in-law—about to be cremated
Swimming pool pupils stalled
Pacemaker heart still pumping
Some blood to body and face

This navy seal was turning another shade
He and I had both worn neutral eyeglasses
That went moderately well with many facial tones

Slabs of color planes crisscrossed
And caught the sunlight that Tuesday hospice morning
And that pacemaker had to be removed before
Cremation to avoid exploding

So that he could backstroke away

My Mother-in-Law's Shower

I offered to wash her, as did her daughter and daughter-in-law
Her breasts had survived breastfeeding and cancer
Those soft cascades of flesh which terraced
to her stomach were now deflated, baby-less arms

Her former self was erect with straight toes—different from now
Her character has been softened
To empty places
Something came and stole her mind
Her late husband's voice used to calm her

She is in and out
Phases of the moon and sea pull
Her to look at
Herself, gently on the inside

Bathing day, water rushed over her
And an actress was found dead in a lake
A year-old baby was shot dead in his stroller
California closed down

Water is rushing, washing at all mistakes

My husband was once curled inside her, waiting, then
I put a patio chair in the shower
Below her, for support
And realized how fragile she was
And she was heavy, I had to do everything
Brace myself to not let her fall

She had to hold onto me too
To hold her was to truly love her again
Differently, for the first time, in years

I never saw her vaginal pass,—but I held her steady enough to move
the
        Bubbled sponge over her private parts

She was not even that dirty
From a world inside of doors

Her blue negligee
Waited at attention, Wildfire
That shower settled part of every family's story—evidence
about how to miss all mothers as they wash away

Five Different Painters' Lines

For Frederick Hammersley
My painter has a giant in him, he is all filled in,
And his flat planes carry me softly, like a wisp caught in the stove
Frederick has several likenesses, like snowflakes and cacti, like
rolling bedrooms.

For Jasper Johns
My neighbor has a bank in him, he is standing nearby,
And he carries me, like a sandwich, to an audience
Johns has several likenesses, like intelligence and the flag, like
impatience.

For Keith Haring
My friend has a generosity in him, he invited me inside his
apartment,
And his red, blue, and yellow walls carry me, like a key lying next
to a rose
Keith has several likenesses, like AIDS and glasses, like Peter Pan
flying away.

For Yves Klein
My idol has a chemical blue to him, he had an opening,
And his friends drank the whiskey punch and carried themselves
home, lying down to sleep
Yves has several incarnations, like the blue they all peed, like a
70's happening to them in their homes.

For Krishna Kulkarni
My mentor has fingerprints in him, he showed me his whispers
and birds,
And his outside and inside life carry me, like lunch he would
make
Krishna is a cloud above, like lungs.

Inventive

the remarkable meeting of the poet last night

one is left behind with wishes for the world
the camisole I wore to bed was not my own
see the deep green funerary urns that decorated the bedroom walls
the name of a play was written across a take-out food carton

somehow the long cuffs of the sleeve managed to escape the fire on the
stove
one should never buy all of one thing—leave one behind
as the frost persists on the blue glass tables outside
the key to my friend's hotel room was still buried at the bottom of my
purse
the windows can't be cleaned
the French fries are left on the street for someone to find

the exhilaration skiers must feel
while winter comes on wet, wild
persimmons perched for my grandmother's Thanksgiving
the wood lectern and how it sounds and looks
noticing a tiny blob of blood on my white blouse
spoilt unlike the Christmas cactus with its watery see through-leaves

November and December about to leave again
names of children and plants
to last until the advent and exhaustion of words

Dedications

"The Beginning Seams of January" is for Andrea Henderson Fahnestock and in memory of George Hambrecht.

"Today My Daughter" is for Janet, June, Winter and our mothers, Janet and Annette.

"Kathmandu" is dedicated to Hilda and the memory of her twin sister, Gilda.

"In the Hospital" is dedicated to Ms. Denalise Ruiz, Ms. Joanna St. Bernard James, Dr. Steven McCormick, Dr. Amanda Hambrecht, Dr. Alan Dechairio, Dr. E. Sander Connolly, Dr. Marc S. Eisenberg, Dr. David Lessman, Dr. B. Janet Hibbs, Dr. Anthony Rostain, Dr. Thomas Magnani., Dr. Robert Rubman, Dr. Rigerio Lobo, Dr. Marc Lemchen, Dr. Amardeep Saluja, Dr. Oscar Shadle, Dr. Raymond Wintroub, Dr. Buz Abrams, Dr. Erico Cardoso, Dr. Elliott Higgins, Dr. David Shlim, Dr. Andrew J. Gerber, Dr. Jonathan Avery, the late Dr. Bruce Barron, and Torrance Memorial Hospital.

"TREES and Besides Us" is dedicated to the work of His Holiness the Dalai Lama, Chokyi Nyima Rinpoche, Phelgye Kelden, Thupten Gelek, and everyone who participated in *The Art of Impermanence*.

"California Dry Tethered" is dedicated to Pamela Salvatore, Marci Stearns, Joyce Corrigan, Lesa Vogliano, Kirstin Cole, Sharman Cole, Marla Malcolm, Jill Brooke, Alison Kaplan, and their mothers, and Christine and Spencer Biddle, and Mike Millius and Ulla Maija Kivimaki.

"House Fire in Chile" is dedicated to Rosie and Chris Spelius and all our friends in Chile, firefighting, and teaching children to swim.

"An About to be Cremated Swimmer" is for Bob Weeden and the American Bird Conservancy.

"My Mother-in-Law's Shower" is for Leslie Weeden and research on Alzhiemers and Dementia.

Additional Acknowledgments

Thank you very much to those people and presses who have published my work and to Christen Kincaid, Leah Huete de Maines, Mimi David, and Kevin Maines. Thank you also to early readers Sara Arnell, Olivia Farr, Sean Singer, Elaine Sexton, Carla Carlson, Brot Coburn, and Susie Boyt.

To a lyric essay class with Carla Carlson at the Writing Institute at Sarah Lawrence.

Carlson had Modigliani's Reclining Nude on the wall as a prompt, which eerily resembled my dying mother's pose and set me off writing.

To the Three Lives & Co Bookstore in NYC, where Rilke's *Letters to a Young Poet* literally fell on my head. Rilke's voice has been kicking around since then, especially the superb translations of his work by Stephen Mitchell.

To my family, friends, and teachers heartfelt thanks: Lisa Johnson, Jefferey Steiger, Molly McBride, Peggy Kennedy, Marla Witteman, Marilyn Glass, Sara and Ed, Didi Thunder, Emanuela Corielli, James Gerard, Lucinda and Robin Parish, Sarah Kowitz, Maggie Simmons, Raewyn Gould, Lisa Oberg, Lyllah Horlander, John Beroud, Linda Singer, Josh Hammer, Darcel Ramirez Hamson, Jennifer Laity, Brot Coburn, Arlene Burns, Ritchie Geisel, Daniel Guillaro, Alan Maca, Bill Nation, Tekla Von Hagke, Diana Cloud Quimby, Lily Arnell, Liz Taggart, Sabina and Harlan Stone, Ruth and Michael Toporoff, Paul Salvatore, John Farr, Maireade Kilgalon, and my fellow writers at 2Horatio, Poetry Apocalypse, other classes and workshops.

To my brother Russell Dymock Smith—a dedicated patron of the arts—who has had an outsized influence on me.

To my husband, Don Weeden, whose support for my work, and mentorship about adventure and the natural world have been immeasurable.

To my son, Jack, who has been, and is the inspiration and influence for almost everything I think and do since we met about 9249 days and nights ago.

Vanessa Hedwig Smith is a painter, filmmaker, and writer who has lived and worked in India, Nepal, England, and the US. She has worked on feature-length documentaries, shorts, PSAs, music videos, outdoor installations, murals, and other design projects. Smith produced a BBC Correspondent which helped free a 14-year old girl from prison, helped to change Nepalese law, and won the Amnesty International Media 2000 Award. She holds a BA from Stanford in Urban Design, and an MA from Columbia University in Anthropology.

Her work can be seen at *http://vanessahsmithpictures.com*

www.ingramcontent.com/pod-product-compliance
Lightning Source LLC
Chambersburg PA
CBHW022056080426
42734CB00009B/1379